PODCASTERS MASTERY

THE DEFINITIVE GUIDE TO BOOSTING YOUR CELEBRITY WITH YOUR VOICE

David Ralph

Published in Great Britain in 2018
Under the **HypnoArts** label by
the Academy of Hypnotic Arts Ltd.
1 Emperor Way, Exeter, EX13QS
Hypnoarts.com

Enquiries should be addressed to the
Academy of Hypnotic Arts.
bookpub@hypnoarts.com

First printed edition 2018
British Library Cataloguing in Publication Data
ISBN Number: 978-1-9998921-9-7

Praise for Podcasters Mastery

Mark Egan - *Mobile Video Expert - Ex BBC journalist*
"I ended up reading this cover to cover in one go. Loved it. Such a simple and easy to digest format. There is no fluff and the some of the advice is the EXACT opposite of what I've heard from others. Learning what you should do from a massively successful podcaster is so valuable...but even more valuable is understanding what you DON'T need to bother with to be a success. This book will keep you focused, inspired and remove any barriers that are keeping you from creating a winning podcast."

~

Lisa Avery - *Positive Psychologist and Confidence Coach*
"Much like David Ralph's personal and podcasting style, this book is brimming with wisdom, insight and a straight-forward practicality that makes it an absolute must for anybody in the podcasting field."

~

Steve Reza - *Knife Makers Mastery*
"No matter who you are, you can take control of your life and scale your free time through the power of podcasting that is the message of David Ralph's book. He is a master at teaching the formula for freedom in a practical, common-sense approach. David is brilliant, honest, raw, and completely authentic. His uncanny ability to be himself is refreshing and

timely! Reading his book felt as though I was sitting in a pub having a chat with a good mate!"

~

Dana Wilde - *Bestselling Author of Train Your Brain and Host of The Mind Aware Show*
"If you want to learn everything you need to know about starting your podcast in ONE afternoon, then look no further. This actual transcript of an interview with David is an easy read, and you'll feel like you've just had a face-to-face conversation with him. The ten easy steps he reveals are the roadmap to launching your podcast and doing it quickly. I wish I would have had this when I started!"

~

John Lagoudakis - *Brisbane's Most Trusted Digital Marketing Agency*
"I just finished reading David Ralph's 'Podcasters Mastery' book. If you want to know EXACTLY what it takes to create a successful podcast, everything you need is right here in this book. What I love about this book is that David doesn't leave anything out, and that he is totally genuine. He tells you what you need to do, and what to stay away from... which will save you a lot of time and money, because it goes against what most people are told to do. I can thoroughly recommend this book. If you want to explode your profile, and get people coming to you, and wanting to work with you, nothing beats podcasting."

Dedication

This book is dedicated to Debbie, Daniel and Ashlee who on a day to day business, I'm sure would wish I didn't use my voice so much....and to all my podcast listeners who have a different point of view......
I couldn't have done it without you!

Contents

Introduction

I'm guessing that you're reading or listening to this because you might feel that you're drifting through life in a lack lustre way and that being an entrepreneur or business owner is no longer connecting you to the life you want, or wanted to live, where every day you wake up with a YAY, rather than a disconsolate sigh.

Or maybe you're still stuck in your corporate cubical life listening to podcasters and knowing you could do that!

Hi, and welcome to **Podcaster's Mastery** - *The Definitive Guide to Boosting Your Celebrity With Your Voice.*

This is Jonathan Chase for HypnoArts Books, and in the interview, which has created this book, I'm privileged to be talking with David Ralph whose podcasting expertise has set hundreds, if not thousands, of entrepreneurs and business owners on the right path to easily grow their business, explode their profiles and bring new and exciting opportunities to their lives and the lives of others.

I'm glad you're here, and so won't miss out on this unique opportunity to learn these skills that David has so generously given in the following pages.

In this book, especially for the entrepreneur and business owner, you'll find that one thing that will re-connect you to your audience to give you more **Free Time**, a **Profile Explosion** and More **Speaking Opportunities**. Here podcasting expert David Ralph, guides you through the sure-fire steps that got him, in just a few years, to the number one business motivational podcaster spot on iTunes, and probably the world.

With a global reach of 5million plus downloads in 138 countries, and an easy online audio marketing solution that doesn't need a team, expensive equipment or even a dress code;

David came from the position you might be in right now, as you'll see from his story a little after this, and can prove that podcasting will leave you hand's free, so to speak, to lead a hassle and stress-free life on your terms.

Carolyn Cole, Host of the Boomtank Business Show says,
"Podcaster's Mastery is outstanding! I now have a successful, global podcast I love, reaching prospective clients and enthusiastic listeners around the globe, who are buying my services. Having the podcast paved the way for me to grow my business much faster, in a defined, targeted way, with authority."

If you follow the steps in Podcasters Mastery you can grow your audience and create more opportunities for yourself than you ever thought possible, and have more lunches with the family too.

As with any learnable skill, most of what you need is instruction and encouragement from someone who's been there and done that. David Ralph is uniquely qualified to help you understand everything you need to know about online audio marketing.

3

What Is Podcasters Mastery?

Jon: David, thank you for sharing your experience with us on this live interview.

David: It's an absolute delight to be here Jon.

Jon: David, in a few words what is **Podcasters Mastery**?

David: Podcasting as a format is quite new and it's something that's taken the world by storm. It's really the ability to connect with people that you wouldn't have been able to connect with previously unless you were phoning them or doing a discovery call or meeting them in a social environment.

Now, you can use your voice, your knowledge, your ability to convey that information via a podcast.

I think podcasting mastery is that ability to get that bridging of the gap, that connection with your ideal client without all the hassle that goes on behind the scenes of creating a podcast.

You know somebody once said, "the ultimate sophistication is simplification" or something like that.

I think it's just finding a simple process to be able to connect with people almost on a one on one basis to convert them into customers.

David's Story

Jon: So, tell us, David, how did you get
           here?

David: It's a funny old story actually
           because it has followed suit
           throughout my life.

           My show is called Join Up Dots,
           where we get the guests to look
           back on their life and see the steps
           that have led them there.

           If I go right back to when I started
           work, people used to hear me talk
           and say, "You should be on radio.
           You'd have a great radio voice."

           So, I dabbled and tried to get into
           radio. I didn't really push it. Wrote

a few letters and stuff, and didn't really do that but it was floating around all the time.

When I got to the end of my corporate life and I just felt jaded and I wanted something to do, I heard a couple of podcasts and I thought, I could do this. This is something that I've got the skills to do.

Now, never in my *wildest* dreams did I realise it would take me to where it has, but that was my starting point.

Now, the interesting thing with this Jon, is, I had to go and clear out my mum's attic once and when I went back, there was a box of cassette tapes, little things that we used to have in the 80's and it had my writing on it when I was about seven or eight and it made me realise that I used to go round with a microphone and interview the bank manager, the butcher and I used to knock on their door and say, "Excuse me, could I interview you?"

This podcasting kind of vibe that I do now has actually been throughout my life.

I've been fascinated with people. I've been fascinated with their stories. I love to tell a story myself, so that's how I got here. It was simply a case of connecting with a passion inside me, which translates really well on a podcast.

That is the beauty with everyone. Every single person has got a story. They've got a *passion* which they can convey on a podcast to actually bring in similar people into their world to once again convert them into customers.

Jon: What was the epiphany for you? What point did you say, "Right, I'm going for this full blast"?

David: I left my corporate job to become a web designer because I can do that quite well. There was a fundamental flaw with it though that after three days of doing it, I realised I *hated* it.

It was all right doing it as a hobby but actually thinking, god, I've got to do this for the rest of my life.

I was at home on my own. There was no one there. The cat wasn't very chatty and so I thought to myself, I'll tell you what, put on a podcast, it's like people are talking in the office.

I listened to three back to back and on the third one, I just had the epiphany of, I could do this. It was nothing more than that. It wasn't like the road to Damascus. It wasn't the clouds opening and angels singing on top of me. It was just the pure thinking of, I think I can do that.

That's when I went for it, as soon as I thought that ...

I kept it secret for a while because I felt a bit embarrassed by it. I felt a bit like, why would anyone listen to you? Who are you to get up? Who are you to do this kind of stuff but I went hell for leather once I thought to myself this is something I can do, and it's been proven because it's become a very lucrative business for me.

What's Going On?

Jon: What in your observation and opinion, what's going on with society and technology and the world in general, that especially entrepreneurs and business owners need to know right now to boost their business?

David: This is the power of podcasting, Jon.

Without a doubt, there is too much going on. There are people tweeting you. There's people YouTubing you. There's people doing blog posts. Every time you click on something, cookies retain your information and keep on bombarding you with it.

The beauty of podcasting, I believe, is that it separates all that noise into a conversation that people focus in on.

The majority of my listeners say to me, I listen to you on the train going to work, or I listen to you in the car. I listen to you mowing the lawn, whatever they do they are actually separating themselves from all that noise, so it becomes doubly powerful.

When you hear somebody's voice in your head, you start to kind of fantasise about actually knowing them. I've done it myself. I've listened to people on the radio and used to think to myself, I could go out for a drink with that person.

That person seems really good or that person seems a real idiot.

Through that connectivity and that intimacy, once again, you drown out all the noise.

You're not focused on the business. You're not focused on what the person is telling you. You're focused on *how* the person is telling you and that builds huge loyalty in every business and that's been the greatest boost to my business.

People listen, they listen, they listen and then they start to trust you, and then they start seeking you out, and then you build up relationships with them and you turn them into customers.

It's the easiest process you can do because there's no hard selling.

That to me is the power of podcasting.

Jon: What's different about society now that people are going back to what's basically a really old idea of listening to the radio?

I understand what you said because I think it was Oscar Wilde said that he "preferred radio, the pictures were so much better".

What's happening in society as far as the technology and everything else? Is there a movement in any specific area at all?

David: I think there's two movements. I think there's a realisation that people like stories. You go back thousands and thousands of years and people were painting stories on cave walls. They were sitting around fires. They were at campsites. They were in marketplaces.

People like stories. If you blend that in with the personal branding, and I think that is the biggest change in business, since I've been in it the last three or four years.

When I started, literally every website didn't have any image of the person behind it. It was all glossy images. It was all Photoshop, but now, every time you go over, you will see pictures of the people with their kids and really rough stories and they share warts and all.

It's the personal branding which is making all businesses thrive.

You're seeing the master of that in Richard Branson at Virgin. Literally every time you see something, it's a picture of him. It's him doing something. You're connecting with the person and not the brand.

Those two things, stories and personal branding are the difference nowadays and I think it's just going to get bigger and bigger and bigger with people connecting with you on video, seeing you having your dinner.

It's becoming like that hybrid of celebrity big brother when you can just sort of ... Voyeurism at its best through business.

What Are The Alternatives?

Jon: We're centred on podcasting here
            but what *are* the alternatives? We
            know online marketing is vital and
            podcasting is one way of achieving
            that. For you it's the best way.
            However, there are other ways, yes?

David: Yeah, there is. There's always other
            ways.

            I love podcasting because it's been
            very good to me and I now know
            exactly the winning formula for a
            podcast but you can take that
            concept into blogging. You can
            take it into YouTube and Facebook

live. Any way that you've got to connect with your tribe, then it will work.

What the problem is Jon, is that so many people have a, *blast everywhere* approach, and they don't consider where their audience is.

What we're talking about here in podcasting and in everything is *gaining traffic* but there's traffic everywhere.

You don't actually have to gain traffic. If you get in your car, every single person that drives past you is traffic. They're customers. They're buying. They're looking. They're shopping.

All you've got to do with all these formats is know where your tribe are hanging out and connect with them.

The beauty of podcasting, I think is, it's easier than anything because there's different ways of actually spreading that information across your tribe, so that they find it and they share.

Any way you want to do it, it's going to work but you've got to know who you're targeting and then you've got to provide the information that will make them want to connect with you.

The difference is, with blogging and ... YouTube and Facebook live would be very similar to podcasting ... but with blogging, it's very difficult to build up that loyalty, so I would never have a blog without some kind of video or audio on it because that is the connectivity. That's the personality. That is where people connect.

But they're all going to work, as
long as you know where your
people are hanging out.

What You Need To Do

Jon: David, if **Podcaster's Mastery** is
            the answer, what do entrepreneurs
            and business owners need to
            know?

            What's the right *mindset or mood or
            even physical state,* for the reader or
            listener of this, when it comes to
            getting started with podcasting
            mastery. Where do they need to
            position themselves to get the most
            out of what's coming next? How
            do we get there?

David: We get there by actually **connecting
            with our inner selves**, really *knowing*
            ourselves. So many people screw
            up big time where they look at

what other people are doing and they go, "Oh, that's working. I'm going to do what that person is doing." So, they create a hybrid of that show and it falls flat. Everyone can hear it's a false routine.

What you *have* to do to get into the right mindset is just imagine you're in a pub. Just imagine that you're talking to somebody one on one. You *just imagine* that there's no recording. It's just you, having a conversation.

That is the real mindset and it takes a while to get there.

I think when I started my show, I was all right but I think I was, *fake it until you make it* kind of thing. I was *playing* at being the podcasting host.

When my show really took off was when I just decided all I was going to do is turn on the microphone and start talking. That's when people once again can get excited by the content.

It's a mindset of *how do I really be myself.* It's a mindset of being authentic. It's also a mindset of… *this has got to be consistent.* It can't just be a one podcast episode and you're going to win the game. This is going to be **content**, **content**, **content** and keep on churning it out.

As we're recording this, I've done nearly 1000 episodes in just under four years and I'm picking up speed. I love it.

The ability to just have these conversations with people and convert them into podcasts, to me, it isn't a churn anymore because it's become easy because I've tapped into that being, my authentic self, and found systems to make it easier for me as well. That just means it's not work anymore.

If you can get to that point, when it doesn't seem like work, I think that you've really hit the podcasting gold.

Jon: Would you say that people should be thinking about being playful, excited?

David: I think they should just be themselves.

There's nothing worse when somebody who's generally really serious and then you listen to them on the podcast and you think what's he doing? It's just got to be who you are. If you're a serious person, then the content is going to be serious.

If you're going to be playful and stupid ... I'm a playful and stupid person so my content comes out that way. I just enjoy doing that. You can't fake it. You can't just be false.

Whoever you are, just try to get that out on the microphone.

For example, if I'm listening to a history podcast, I want somebody that sounds quite serious. That's just what I want with that. If I'm listening to something sports based, I want somebody to be more excited because that's what you get with sport.

It's all got to tie up with your personality and the content and don't fake it. If you fake it, you'll be dead before you start. People will pick up on that and they will swap.

What they will do, if you are trying to become your *authentic* self, they will stick with you. They can sense that. I've done it myself.

There's some podcasts that I go back to time and time again because I just know the person is being real, and I like that realism in everything that I listen to.

Jon: It's that word of authenticity that seems to be about so much nowadays.

David: Yeah, I think it's true and that's what ties up with the personal branding. That is everything about it. Being authentic so people can make that decision, whether they want to get into a relationship with you, financially, socially or whatever.

Authenticity is the key to everything now. It has to be because you've got to be as real as you possibly can, otherwise these people won't ever connect with you.

It's not like they're going to meet you in a pub, three or four times and actually think you're all right.

You've really just got to lay it out and the people that do like you, will like you and the people that hate you, they'll go off somewhere else.

Never worry about them, just worry about being yourself and connecting with the people that like who you are.

Ten Steps To Starting Your Podcast
Step 1: Finding Your Perfect Audience

Jon: This is the how-to section. Okay David, what's the first thing you want people to do when they start their podcast?

David: The very first thing you need to do is actually not focus in on the audience at all.

            You focus in on yourself.

            We've already spoken about this but there's no point in creating a podcast that you get bored with

and you just think I can't be
bothered to do this. *You've got to find
the subject that's right for you.*

So many people talk about creating
your perfect avatar, which I'm
going to talk about in a moment,
because it is vitally important to
know who wants to listen to your
content, but you've got to decide
whether you are going to be able to
provide 1000 episodes, 8000
episodes or after seven episodes,
you dry up. That is the biggest
failing that I see.

When I talk to podcasters that have
started and have stopped, they all
say, "I got bored with doing it."

Now, I love doing it because I
chose a subject that I'm fascinated
with. I'm fascinated with people's
success stories. I'm fascinated with

how they're getting there and the
dots that join up. You've *got* to
know yourself first.

Once you've got that understanding
of what you actually will be
interested in talking about, then
you've *got* to think about the
audience and you've *got* to think
about where they are and start
researching them.

I always recommend that you
spend a week, two weeks, three
weeks looking at creating the
perfect avatar you can,
understanding their *pain points*, their
pleasure points, the things they're
talking about, the things that they
want to know about because
ultimately with a podcast, it's
about getting them to open their
wallets up.

There's no point in doing it as a hobby. Well, I suppose you could do it as a hobby…but I wouldn't.

I always think that you've got to understand your customer and understand what they are ultimately going to need help with and pay for, so *you need* to get into Facebook groups. *You need* to get into forums. *You need* to understand what they are having trouble with and start building your content around that.

The *first step* is actually two steps. Know yourself but know your customer better than they know themselves and then you're on to a winner.

Jon: How would you in a practical way, just give me a couple of paragraphs, actually go about doing that?

David: The first thing is, I would look at myself. (*I actually have a 10-part video course that I provide to my tribe about this*), but in simple terms, you can get a piece of paper and draw three lines down it so there's **three columns**.

❖ In one column, you have LOVE.

❖ The second one, you have LIKE.

❖ the third one, you have HATE.

Over about a three-week period, every time you go to do something... and it can be silly things like watching EastEnders, and you think, *I hate this*. Put EastEnders in the hate bit. Washing up! *Hate this*. Now, going for walks. *I love this*.

You will start to have themes.

You will have themes running through it and if there's a lot of stuff about being outside and nature, then that's going to be a great podcast episode for you to start recording about.

That would really be the first step and then you can drill down, you can go onto Google. You can have a look around and wonder why am I enjoying that so much? Why am I enjoying being outside? How can I make money on talking about being outside?

There's always about eight income streams for every subject that you start podcasting about. That would be the first step. Do your, love, like, hate's and *really* work out what subject you adore like no other.

Secondly, with the customer, you need to, as I say, go where your customer is.

If you have decided that you want to do a podcast on the great outdoors, I would go onto camping sites and camping forums and nature trails and anywhere you think that people are hanging out and talking and join those Facebook groups. Join those forums and start chipping in and look for the questions.

Every time somebody poses a question, that is where they need an answer. If they've got an answer, they will likely pay for a quick transformation to where they want to be. Get enough of those and you're already building products that you can build into your money platforms on your podcast. Does that make sense?

Jon: Yes, absolutely. Basically, you're looking for the person who's asking the right question.

David: Yeah. You're asking the question where they are, pretty much ... It's the **how**, **why**, **what**.

If somebody is doing a car podcast for instance and somebody says, "What's the quickest way that I can get my car to go to 130 miles an hour?" If you get a few of those, you might want to create a video course showing people how they can do that.

It's all the questions and if there's enough questions, they're telling you that they're going to pay for solutions, so you get the traffic and build little bite sized products here or there, that is where the money starts.

It's great to earn money from your podcast straightaway and I believe that from the first listener you should be able to.

Step 2: Set Up Your Platform

Jon: What's the next step, the second step that people should do?

David: The second step is actually starting to **set up your platform**. A lot of people get hung up on the microphone and the mixer and all the technical aspects. I always say to them, if you can talk into a phone, you're a podcaster already.

That is basically what it is. All you're doing is you're pressing record and you're keeping that voice so that you can share it with other people.

You do need to buy a microphone. You do need to buy a mixer. Very cheap. No more than 100 dollars to set yourself up and then you have to buy a hosting account.

What a hosting account is, is you record a file on your computer, an MP3 file.

It doesn't stay on your computer.

You give it to a company who then gives you a little link and that link is what you share with the world. When somebody clicks on that link, it then plays on the hosting account and they will start sharing that podcast around the world.

That is it, simply. You talk into a microphone, through a mixer, onto a recording device. You create a little file and you pass it to the world and you shouldn't spend more than 100 dollars to start podcasting.

It's very, *very* cheap and you, literally within the first month, you should've got your money back if you're doing it right.

Jon: I know you have a studio but you can do it from a bedroom or anywhere.

David: Yeah. You can do it absolutely anywhere. There's some very good podcasts out there that people do when they're driving in their car. There's people that do it on aeroplanes!

One of my favourite podcast episodes was two podcasters chatting on a plane. They had time to kill, so they connected their microphones up to a little recording device and they just spoke.

For a podcaster, hearing two podcasters talking about their business and how they're doing it, it was brilliant. You don't have to set yourself up in really flashy ways. *You do have to be aware of audio issues though.*

If you're in a house and somebody's running around and the only room you can get is right by the toilet, it's probably not the best place to record.

You've got to think about, how you can get the best audio?

I even know people that sit in their cupboard with clothes all around them. That actually is a brilliant place. You get perfect podcasting sound by opening your wardrobe, crouching in at the bottom with your laptop or whatever and just talking straight into it. It's amazing how you can do it. Even under your bed, you can climb under your bed and do it.

Jon: Is that because dining rooms and offices tend to be echo-y?

David: Absolutely. Absolutely.

At the moment, I'm recording raw, as I say. I'm not doing anything for the ambiance of the room.

If you come into a bathroom, it's echo-y because it's all flat walls. You don't have curtains and stuff. You go into a lounge that hasn't got furniture in it, it's going to be echo-y.

The more stuff you get into a room, the more it dampens the sound. If you're in an office, generally it's always going to be more echo-y and it's not the best place to do podcasting.

You've got to find a very small place where you can dampen the sound. Even, and I teach my students this, even recording with a towel over your head will do wonders for your audio. It will just stop the sound from bouncing off the walls and coming back to the microphone.

You can't hear it yourself really but on a recording, it just takes it into that amateur zone. You might look stupid with a towel over your head but it's not about what you look like because no one can see you recording anyway. It's what the audience gets to listen to.

Step 3: A Winning Launch

Jon: David, what's the third step and
         how do we do it?

David: I've learned this from experience
         but I think a ***winning launch*** is
         about holding back until you are
         ready to launch the *right way*.

         I started Join Up Dots and I did an
         hour plus episode seven days a
         week for a whole year. Literally I
         was chasing all the time to get
         content in. "I'm running out. I've
         only got two more shows to go.
         I'm running out".

         The biggest step that I would say is
         first of all define your audience and

how much content they need you to deliver.

If it's somebody doing a podcast on real estate, for example, it might be perfectly acceptable to do an episode a week. That might be perfectly right for the audience. If it's somebody who's doing something on public speaking, similar.

You've got to really understand *how much content* you want to produce for your audience and then start recording that content.

I would say get about 30 episodes recorded *before* you launch. It gives you a great buffer and it means that you're not pressurised, that you think you're going to run out like I was.

It was a real horrible situation. I was just thinking, it's all going pear shaped here. I can't stop it.

Now, how we do this is, we basically just record in either solo or we record by finding guests and bringing them on the show and telling them that it is a pre-record. It will be going out at a later stage.

You can define when it's going to launch and then build up your launch team.

What I mean by that is you can say to all your friends, all your family, you can say to everyone on Facebook, I'm launching a podcast on this day. If I drop a link in on the day, would you listen to it? Would you go over to iTunes and leave a rating and review? Because iTunes ratings and reviews are *absolutely gold* and they will start pushing you up the rankings.

More often than not, a new podcast can quite easily hit number one on iTunes because so many people are leaving ratings and reviews because they're getting the ball rolling.

That would be my three steps really. My **third step is three steps**.

First of all, I would decide on the amount of content you're going to provide for your customer.

Secondly, I would get a block of work done before I decide to launch.

Thirdly, I would get all my friends and family to be ready for it so that on the day, in the first week, they can jump across, they can click a link, they can listen and they can leave *ratings and reviews*. **That's the gold** and that will set your podcast apart from everyone else.

Jon: Do people cheat at that? Do they set up false names and that sort of thing and put lots of reviews in?

David: I suppose they could. It's going to be difficult though because you've got to add a different address. You've got to have a credit card. You can't just open an iTunes account. You've got to open an iTunes account and put credit card details in. If I've got hundreds of credit cards, I suppose I could but who does?

Jon: The reviews we read are genuine?

David: I think that they're genuine. Unless somebody tells me otherwise... In the old days actually, there was a company on Fiverr, that you could go across to and pay for reviews ... I don't know how they did it but you could pay for a lot of reviews, but iTunes wised up to that and they slammed them.

All the podcasts that were high because of these fake reviews dropped like a stone and they disappeared.

I would say that unlike Amazon and places, I would say iTunes reviews are pretty damn as close as possible to being genuine. I can't imagine that somebody would go to that much effort to create fake ones.

Step 4: Grow Your Audience

Jon: David, what's the fourth step? How
         do we grow our audience?

David: One of the reasons that I love
         podcasting, is that you can grow an
         audience easily, and the best way
         that you can do that with, is with
         iTunes.

         We really need to *understand
         everything* about iTunes as this is the
         home of podcast lovers. They're
         looking for your content. You've
         just got to find the *right way* of
         getting them to find your content.

         Actually, in my online course,
         Podcaster's Mastery, that's the big

block of work. That is the most powerful part of everything.

Away from that, you once again need to find out where your audience is and start posting that content to them.

I used to do Facebook, Pinterest, Instagram, Twitter. Used to do all these places and I stopped doing them one by one because I realised actually I was just giving the wrong content to the wrong people.

So, it comes back again, Jonathan, to *know your customer*. I can't emphasise that enough. You know your customer. You know where they are. You know that they're going to want your content and they will know people that like your content as well because they're in those groups and you deliver directly.

Focus in on those and you will start to grow your audience. But, if you want a big blast of audience, you've *got* to understand iTunes. 600 million people on iTunes. 600 million active podcast listeners on iTunes. That's where the gold is and I cannot emphasise that enough.

Once I changed my focus from a 'blast everywhere' approach to just focusing 100% on iTunes, my audience went up and up and up and up.

Jon: Is there anything that you do or say in your actual podcasts like CTA's, call to action, that you do openly or subtly that helps the listener to want to further your podcast, through recommending getting other people to listen.

David: I do but it doesn't overly work. People just generally don't do stuff that you say on a podcast. They have to *want* to do something.

Where I find a great way of doing it is when somebody does connect with me on Facebook to ask me a question, I will *always* record an audio voicemail, send it back to them and at that time, I will *always* say if you could leave a rating review or if you could tell your friends about it and they seem to do it.

I do that because I've actually given them something back, I've given them personalised value, even though the podcast is value and I've *spent time* recording it for them, that *one on one, doing something for them*, they *do something back*. It's the reciprocation rule. That is really, *really* powerful.

Whenever anybody connects with me, I always say a little bit cheeky but this is the podcaster's mantra, "If you could leave a rating review on iTunes, I would really appreciate it" and more often than not, they go, "Yeah, no problem at all. Thanks for your help, David. I'll go and do that" and they do.

I do occasionally say at the end of the show, "Thank you very much for listening. If you know anybody who'd be interested in my content, share it."

But I know what it's like. People generally share bad news and they don't share good stuff, so it's not the juicy thing to say, "I'm listening to this. I'm listening to that."

But as soon as anyone connects with you, which they will do on

Facebook, ***over deliver*** back to them. It's really quick. You don't have to write War and Peace on an email. I just record straight into my microphone, send a message out to them, using an online link generator called 'voicespice.com' and they get my *voice* in their email.

They've actually connected with the podcast host and they always will do something back for me. That's how I do it.

Step 5: Get Your Audience To Connect

Jon: What's the next step, David?

David: The next step is basically making it
            as easy as possible for them to
            connect with you. I've said to
            people, if you want to send an
            email, but people can't be
            bothered. I've said to people, if
            you want to tweet, people do, but
            it's quite hard to monitor.

            All I do with mine is, I say to
            people, send a message through on
            Facebook and they do. I love
            Facebook and I hate Facebook as
            well.

On the personal side, I never go on it. I don't do anything personal at all on Facebook but for my business, that is how I connect.

They send a message through to Join Up Dots at Facebook and any of the listeners out there, or readers, can test this and they will get an instant message back saying **"Thank you so much, we will connect with you as soon as possible. If you'd like free coaching, then click on this link**." Then they can come into a group that *I'm in every single day.*

That's a good way of building up a relationship.

Then I respond back to them and send that personalised message but you've got to think how is the easiest way for them to do it. If somebody can tell me there's something easier than Facebook, I don't know. It's Facebook messenger that I use and I'm big on responding back as soon as possible, as personalised as possible.

You can use any tool that's right for your business. You can use any tool that's right for your audience and you've *got to know your audience.*

If they're a very old audience, then Facebook seems to be the thing that people like.

If they're a very young audience, people are going onto Snapchat and twitter and some of the other social media but it's got to be as easy as possible for them.

Step 6: Master iTunes

Jon: Having been through your training,
           I've got to say this is gold. David,
           how do we **master iTunes**?

David: Well you master iTunes really by
           buying my course. That's the
           flippant answer but away from that,
           the way you master it is you spend
           time looking at iTunes based
           around the fact that iTunes is a
           search engine.

           iTunes is nothing different than
           Google. It's nothing different from
           Yahoo, Bing, or any of the others.
           It's a place where content is stored
           and where you will go to find that
           content.

If you keep that in your head, it's a big step forward that you can learn and you can go deeper and deeper.

The more knowledge you gain, you will do very, *very* well on iTunes, but if you think about it, it's not about being *found*, it's about being *searched* for.

Make it easy for your audience to search for you and you will start to grow an audience.

That's really the bulk of my whole course in a snapshot. It's that one phrase.

You've really got to think about how can I make my show *be searched* for as *easily* as possible? If you do that, you'll do really well.

Now, I will say I don't actually do

anything else other than what I can do on automatic pilot now. I don't go onto Facebook and post. It just goes automatically on there. I don't go onto twitter. I don't go onto LinkedIn.

Anything other than iTunes, I don't actually do and I've got one of the biggest podcasts out there at the moment and it's all from this simple concept.

Understand iTunes. 600 million people on there. You only need to find your audience and the audience that is looking for your content and make your content as easy as possible to be found.

Jon: That includes, what? Titles, descriptions, that sort of thing?

David: Yeah, everything on iTunes has a

searchable function, basically...or at least most of it does. The titles, absolutely. The description, the author bar. Every single thing on there that can be searched on, should be used.

By using the search bar function at the top right-hand side of iTunes you can find a podcast of your choice. I would advise the readers and listeners to test it out.

Go over there and type in the word 'History' and you will get history podcasts appearing.

You can type in 'Fishing', you would get the same thing. What you've got to do is this. You've got to think about every episode you do. How can you create a title, a description that somebody is likely to type in.

Once again, we keep on coming back to the same thing.

You need to know your customer better than they know themselves, and then you will know what they're going to type in. What they're interested in. You create the content that they're interested in and allow them to find it. It's as simple as that.

On my show, somebody used to rock up as a guest. Then I used to record the show and choose a title afterwards but now I do some research beforehand, to decide on the content that I'm going to talk to the guest about, because I know that people are looking for that content and I *frame my content* based around that.

I've gone a different way. I now know that it's going to be searched for, so I create the content so that when somebody does listen to it, it's relevant to that and it's not just, "hang on, this has got nothing to do with fishing, why is it called fishing?" That's how I do it.

Step 7: Automate Your Podcasts

Jon: So, David, how do we automate podcasts?

David: That is the beauty of podcasting. It is so easy to automate it. Now, of course, you can't get away from the fact that you will have to be the voice of your podcast, so you can't automate that. *You can't get a voice recording of you. It's got to be you.*

            You've got two choices. You've got a solo show, which is brilliant because you can do it whenever you want, wherever you want. You can record it. Take that file and then hand it to the hosting company and on the day that you decide that you want it to be released, it will do the releasing, and out to Facebook, LinkedIn, podcasters, whatever... it goes.

You've literally got the world as your oyster in that regard.

Away from that, you've got the guest coming on to record an interview. That is something that is a little bit more difficult because you've got to find a time that is right for you and a time that's right for your guest and of course when you're recording across the world, there's time zones as well to consider.

I use something called Calendly, which is a booking link system and basically, I just send a link out to the guest. They click on it from their end. I click on it from my end and it sorts out all the times. That's as automated as you need to get.

Away from everything else, every single system out there will have a scheduling programme on it.

You can schedule stuff on Facebook. You can schedule stuff on Linkedin. You can schedule wherever you want on most things.

I actually only do **Join Up Dots** two days a month and everything else, I just turn off and it's almost like I'm not a podcaster but I just roll up and just check and it has gone live, so you can automate everything, even emails to the guests that goes out on automatic.

I set it up straight after I've recorded the show. 'Thank you very much for being on.' I tell the email device what day I want that to go out on and then bang, on that day, it goes out.

You can automate everything. The only thing you can't automate is yourself. You've got to get organised in that regard.

Step 8: Inviting Top Guests

Jon: How do we go about inviting top guests and who are they?

David: When you start a podcast, it is a little bit difficult to get people to come on the show. It's not impossible because I've done it, but it is a little bit more difficult.

When you actually get a winning podcast, you can't stop them. People are just coming to you left, right and centre. It's a **tsunami**.

But how you actually do it is first of all, you write out to them and you say to them, '*I am starting a podcast. I really love your work. I really love what you've been doing recently,* XYZ.' Let the guest know that you are *invested* in them. You're not just doing a spammy email out and '*I would love you to be a guest on my show to really launch it big.*'

That's how I did it. I sucked up to them in the invitation at the very beginning and said, "*Without your help, this show is not going to be what it's going to be. Please help me get going.*" More often than not, you will get a positive response.

The very first day I sent an email, the very first email that I sent was to **Elton John**, funnily enough. I knew I would never get a response but I just knew that it would get me over that obstacle of going, "Oh god, who's going to respond to me?" I thought, go to somebody really famous.

I sent it out. Two seconds later, I sent out another email to a guy, Saturday afternoon and he responded within 30 seconds. "Sounds good" he told me. Didn't even ask what the show was about.

He didn't ask anything. He just said yes because people know that podcasts will live forever and that is constant traffic coming to their site.

It's also a brilliant back link because on your show notes, you will have a link to their website. The more links you get to a website, the higher Google ranks it. It's not that hard to get good guests on.

The trick is to then start playing them against each other.

When you get somebody on like **Jack Canfield,** the *Chicken Soup For The Soul* guy, on the show you need to use his name as leverage. I can then say to people, *"I had Jack Canfield on the show. He loved it. He actually said that you might be a good person to have."*

This is a classic technique that Bob Geldof, (for live aid) used, where he went up to David Bowie and said, "David Bowie, you've got to be on the show" and Bowie would say, "Who else is on there?" He'd say, "Oh I've got Paul McCartney. I've got Queen" and so Bowie would think, 'I'd better be on that'.

Then he'd go to Paul McCartney and say, "Oh, I've got Bowie on the show" and he was just playing them off against each other so that they felt duty bound to appear.

That's how I did it in the very early days.

I had people like **Jason Lewis**. You may not have heard of him but he was the first guy to walk single handed around the earth. Took him 13 and a half years.

I had **Cathy O'Dowd**, first lady to hit both sides of Everest, who's become a great friend of the show and she refers me guests constantly.

Once you get these people on your show and they know that you are good, then they like to share it as well.

So, you get, as I say, a tsunami of guests. I'm absolutely booked out until six or seven months ahead of schedule now. I've actually had to close down the amount of recording that I do because otherwise I'd be three years ahead of schedule.

That's how you do it right in the very first stage, get over yourself and send out requests.

Don't be frightened about sending an email out but do your research.

Tell them that you *love* their work, the reasons why you like their work and then say that they're going to be a big help as you boost your show and I promise you, you will probably get more yes's than no's because they're looking for those google links and constant traffic.

They're looking at another way of brand exposure. It's a real win/win.

Jon: Do you pick specifically guests that have got a fan base that matches yours?

David: Not anymore. There was a time that I did that but now I'm so skilled at podcasting, I can take the content wherever I want to match *my* fan base.

I'm very interested in people's struggles. I'm very interested in their trials and tribulations. I literally will get pitched a guest that comes through and if I look at it and I think "*I've had too many of these,*" then I will draw a line.

At one point I was getting so many business coaches, it was untrue and started saying no to them. Then I started to think to myself, okay, they might be a business coach but they've got a different story.

It's up to me to actually get that out so I won't talk about what they want to talk about. I'll talk about what I want to talk about and go that way. So, I do that now, and I'm not too selective on it.

Where we are with Join Up Dots now, we're having a big rebrand and I am looking to get more, I suppose, celebrity guests on, which is going to be more appealing.

If you scroll through iTunes, a lot of the times you will pick names that you know.

You'll look at people and you go, "He's being interviewed. I'll listen to that."

That's what I'm aiming for now but the whole branding had to match up so that when the celebrities come across, they realise that it's not just a starting website but I control the show.

I control every element of it, so if somebody is going to come onto my show, they talk about what *I* want them to talk about, and I don't really allow them to pitch books and plug stuff. It's very much my show now.

Jon: How much do you manage your actual guests with audio, with telling them what questions you're going to be asking, that sort of thing?

David: I do send an email out a week beforehand and I say to them, first of all, you better listen to some of the shows because they're not your normal shows.

I will go anywhere on my content, anywhere that I fancy and in the early days, it was quite obvious that people hadn't listened to the show. Now, people do.

Not only do they listen to one. They say, "I've listened to six or seven" and they start telling me episodes that they really like. That makes it a lot easier but on the actual week of the show, I send them an overview of the vibe that I'm aiming to create.

If they haven't got a good microphone, I tell them where to go and buy one and I send them a link. I send them a request for the social media that they want me to promote, any pictures.

The only thing that I do myself, I do my intros. I write the introduction. I don't allow the guest to tell me what they want me to lead them onto the show with. That is my thing.

In the early days, I used to do all that, hunting around for the websites and the Linkedin profiles and stuff.

Now, I just ask for it and say, "If you want to come on the show, you've got to do that. If you want to come on the show, you've got to leave a rating review on iTunes. You've got to have a good microphone. If you haven't, we're not going to record."

It doesn't happen very often but sometimes a guest connects and I say to them, "I'm not recording here. This doesn't sound good enough. It's got to be good audio."

I'm allowing some to go past. I had a musician on the show that was actually on tour so he was in a car, driving, with lorries going past and I actually thought, I like that because he's on tour. It's the audio of being on tour so I allowed that to go past.

Other than that, you've got to keep control of your guests all the time because they will try to push you around.

Not the big celebrity ones. The real famous ones, they're good, they're great and they're really professional and they turn up and they're just like putty in your hands.

It's the ones who think they're better than they are, the sort of upward guests. They're the ones that think that they can control you, so you've got to take that firm step right at the very beginning.

Step 9: Become An Expert Broadcaster In Record Time

Jon: David, obviously big question. How does one become an expert broadcaster?

David: You become an expert broadcaster by not listening to podcasts.

I think that's the key.

A lot of podcasts out there are rubbish. They sound rubbish. The content sounds rubbish. The people are just doing it to try to make a quick buck.

What you need to do, is to listen in to the top guys and more often than not, that's on old media. You need to get in and listen to the people on the BBC or whatever radio station you listen to, and really understand what you like about them, how they actually express the enthusiasm they bring into their voice.

Now, on a podcast that I do, I'm very up. I'm like 75% more up than I am in normal life because there's no body language. It's all got to be in the *voice*. It's too high for normal living but it works well on a podcast.

Now I have got three or four experts that I listen to a lot. One of them is a guy called **Howard Stern** in America.

A lot of the English people don't know him but Howard is a genius at asking difficult questions and still getting the answer from the guest. You really have to look at how he phrases the question, how, if the guest doesn't quite answer, he goes again a different way ... He keeps on chipping away, chipping away until the guest feels they have to answer it. He's one that I really look at.

Another guy that I look at, he's not around anymore really, called Michael Parkinson in the United Kingdom. He was a genius interviewer. He allowed the conversation to flow and the third one I would go for is really a podcaster that you like.

Go with the external ones first of all. Think why do I like him? Is the audio good? Is the flow good? Is the content good? Is it short and punchy? Is it long and in depth? That's how you need to do it, but

the key way, is to listen back to
yourself.

I have so many people that I train
or I start to train that say, "Oh, no
I don't listen to myself. I don't like
my voice." If you don't like your
voice, then why should anybody
else like your voice. You've got to
listen back to yourself.

I've done 1000 shows and I would
say I must've listened to my shows
now probably 10,000 times. I listen
to every episode. I listen multiple
times. I listen to how I've done the
intro. Have I stumbled over words?
Does it flow? Do I ask questions
that the guest has to go, "Sorry,
you're asking ..."?

I used to do long questions and
when I used to listen back, I used
to think no wonder the guest was

confused. There's like three questions within that, so they needed a summary. They needed clarification.

Listen back to yourself. Listen like you're studying for an MBA because you will realise all those little weird things that you do, that actually make your broadcasting natural. They're the things you need to emphasise.

I am particularly stupid on the microphone. Not in interview sense but actually on a solo show, I try to be as stupid as possible because that is my natural self.

That's how you do it. Study the good people. Ignore the bad people but study yourself better than anyone.

Jon: Practise?

David: ***Practise, practise, practise***. The
            beauty about it is every time you
            practise, it's a podcast episode. So,
            I don't actually edit at all. I just
            press record and I talk and away I
            go.

            People say to me, "I have to edit all
            my shows, all the um's and ah's
            and everything out there." I always
            say to them, "Don't edit the show.
            Edit yourself. Focus on how you're
            talking and if you're saying um's
            and ah's, try to stop that. Naturally,
            you will."

            I can talk for hours and hours and
            hours and hours and I hardly say
            an um and ah really because it's just
            something I've trained myself to
            do. Yes, fortunately I was a public
            speaker beforehand, so it was

slightly easier but ***don't edit your show, edit yourself.*** Practise, practise, practise. Record. Throw it out to the world.

Don't be too precious about your content either, because you're going to get better anyway.

I've never not released a show. Everything I've ever spoken into a microphone has become a show and it goes out to the world.

Step 10: Podcast Yourself To Your Sexy best

Jon: The final step, which is the one that made me smile when you told me this title is; **podcast yourself to your sexy best.**

David: Yeah. Podcast yourself to your sexy best. You've got to be *bigger* than yourself. You've got to be the person that *you want to be*. It's the person that makes you smile when you listen to them. It's the person that makes a joke and even though it's a stupid joke, it's a cringey joke, you actually smile at yourself.

It's about fascinating on a podcast. It's about intriguing. It's about becoming more interesting than you normally are.

The beauty with a podcast is that it's all voice.

People *only listen to your voice*. They don't see that you're scratching yourself. They don't see that you're leaning back. They don't see all of the body language that we pick up in normal life and we look at people and we make these decisions. ***It's all down to your voice.***

You've really got to set the bar high on that one. You've really got to go for it. Don't be precious about yourself but fascinate yourself. Really enjoy yourself.

I actually laugh a lot when I listen back to my own shows, which it sounds silly to say, but I listen back because what I'm saying may not be funny but I know why I was doing it. I was creating a mood on the show to make it more rounded.

You can do it. *You can be your sexy best.* You can throw away the shackles that say society and environment mean I should be like this. You can just go mad. You can go crazy. You can do anything you want.

Some people will swear on the shows and stuff. I don't because I always think I don't know where it's going to land. Somebody might be listening to it with their kids.

I never swear on my show but away from that, I will do anything I possibly can because it's about fascinating.

Once you start fascinating your audience, you can't stop it. They're going to come back to you time and time again.

They see you as somebody that is doing something that they would *like* to do. They see you as somebody that is a more interesting version of themselves.

In real life, you might be as boring as they are but you don't do that on the microphone. You become *sexy, sexy, sexy* and literally make love to the microphone. Be your *real* self and then push it out to the world.

Jon: If somebody is stuck with the idea of being bigger than themselves, what would you suggest their approach be?

David: Practise. Just practise and listen back to yourself. When you start, you are quite subdued.

If you listen to my shows now compared to the very first episode, the energy isn't there. I thought I was doing it. I thought I was being energised. I thought I was really putting myself into it. I realise now looking back, I wasn't. The only way you can get this is by doing it.

I remember recording the first couple of episodes and thinking that's pretty good. That's okay. Then when I got to episode 37 and I remember this distinctly, I started taking the mickey, making fun of the guests and the guests started responding back in a similar way and I thought ah, this is it. I've started to bill this.

Then I got to episode 100 and I remember I went up again, where I just suddenly realised what is required to run a show. I think I've gone 37, 100, 200, 500 ... 500 was a big landmark episode for me because I thought god, I've done 500 episodes here. It's just going up and up.

You will get stuck if you try to force it to happen but if you just keep on doing it constantly, you'll know when it happens. You'll just feel better. You'll just feel more engaged and you will realise once you've closed that door behind you, you can never go back.

That's your new version. That's your sexy best. That's where you've got to.

Mistakes, Myths and Misunderstandings to Avoid

Jon: What are the biggest Mistakes and misunderstandings to avoid in your opinion?

#1 Mistake: Replicating Another Show

David: Replicating another show is the number one mistake. Absolutely. It is so beyond the number one mistake that it's probably the hundredth mistake, it's the thousandth, it's the infinity mistake.

People listen to other people doing a show and think they only have to replicate that to be a success.

That is totally wrong.

That person has created that show by putting themselves into it. It's become *their* format. I was very lucky. When I started **Join Up Dots**, I didn't really listen to any other podcasts. I listened to maybe three.

When I started doing it, I realised certain things that I needed to do from being a trainer in the old days. *Have a big start. Have a big finish and try to keep the people interested in the middle.* That's the way that I do Join Up Dots.

There's always a big end so people know it's coming to an end. There's a big start and then the middle bit will meander, but it was always my thing.

I knew that I just needed to create my own thing. I didn't follow suit. I didn't do the same sound clips. I just played and had fun and it has become my thing now.

The beauty of that is, if you do your own thing, really put yourself into it, it's very hard for somebody to nick it from you. It's your format. If somebody does, they will say, "Oh, they're doing a David Ralph, or they're doing a Jonathan." It's totally your thing.

Never listen to somebody else and think that you have got to do the same show.

Caveat to that, if they're doing a subject that you really like, then fine, do that. Just do that subject and then put your own spin on it. Put your own sound on. Mess around on there. Make it formal, whatever you want to do but never replicate another show and if you do, I'm going to come around and throw wet flannels at you because that's number one.

#1 Myth: Podcasting Is Hard

Jon: David, what's the biggest myth that most often causes entrepreneurs and business owners to fail completely with podcasting before they even start?

David: A lot of people think podcasting is hard like it's some kind of technological wizardry that you really have to master. **You don't.**

We already said in the book that if you can talk on the phone, you can podcast. It's only putting your mouth out there. I will say to anyone out there. I can teach you in five minutes to be a podcaster. Simple. It really is.

Away from that, there's stuff to learn, to become as good as possible. We can all learn to drive a car very quickly but then meandering your way round all the other idiots on the road is a bit more difficult. That takes the time.

It's exactly the same with a podcast. You can create your own podcast and do very well if it's no competition, but I never use the word hard. It's not hard technically. It's not hard energy wise if you decide on the right content that's right for you and for your guest. It's not hard on getting your show out to the audience, if you know where your audience is.

It's just not hard but people make it hard because they've either been trained the wrong way or they just had this mindset that it's just going to be hard.

It's like all things. If we think that we're going to dislike it, we're going to dislike it. If we think it's going to taste horrible, it's going to taste horrible. It's all mindset at the beginning but believe me, if I can do it, anyone can do it.

#1 Misunderstanding: You Need A Team Behind You

Jon: I know you train a lot of entrepreneurs and business owners, myself included. What do you see as their biggest misunderstanding, that thing where you think in their minds they're actually doing the right thing? The wrong thing, they don't realise it's a misunderstanding.

David: One of the things that I see is delegation.

I was interviewing a podcaster yesterday and he's got a very successful show and he was saying, "I've never edited a podcast in my life." I was saying to him, "Well, nor have I." He said, "Oh, you get somebody else to do it for you?" I say, "No, I just don't edit. I just record and put it out to the world and that's it."

A lot of people think that they need external help. A podcast is really cheap to do. Really, really cheap. Best thing for your business without a doubt, but if you're spending all your money on support, instead of actually finding good ways of doing it for free or using systems, then it's going to become very expensive.

I see a lot of people launch a podcast and think that they've got to have this person editing, this person doing promotion, this person doing this, this person doing that and they say to me, "I had to give up because it's too expensive." I always say to them, "Well, then you're an idiot because you didn't look at the actual concept of what you were doing.

All you're doing is getting yourself into a recording and out to the world." *That's all it is*.

You don't have to have a team behind you. You don't have to have a big empire supporting you.

It's the theme of the whole book.

You just have to know where your tribe is and give them that content. Simple as that. You then don't have to worry about promotional material.

I used to do Twitter. I used to do Facebook images. I used to spend all this time doing all this other stuff. It literally killed me. It was dreadful, so I don't do any of it at all now.

I train people to look at where the tribe is but focus in on what you can do for free because you're always in control of it then. It's brilliant. You can just walk away from it. You can do it when you want. It's totally your show.

Join Up Dots is a global show. Really successful. I do every single thing myself.

There's not one thing that anybody else helps me with and it hardly takes any time at all.

If I can do it, you can.

Massive Motivations

Jon: What are the three real rewards that
          people can get from this? What's
          the first real reward you can see
          that people should get from your
          books and your trainings?

Scaling Your Free Time

David: Scaling your free time. Without a
          doubt, the biggest change in my
          life, I could argue the money and
          all that kind of stuff, but the
          biggest thing for me is my *free
          time*. I always had to do a job
          when the job needed to be done.
          People were always telling me,
          you've got to be there at 9:00. You
          can't leave until 5:00. You've got to

do this, you've got to do that. With a podcast, when you're the host, *you control the time.* You control when people record with you. You control when you record. You control when you push it out.

All my stuff is done when it's suitable for me, leaving me a blank canvas to do what I want with. I am really nailed down on that, and Jonathan, being able to say, it's quite difficult to get me tied down to anything unless I want it to be tied down on, because free time is so important.

If you've got a business and you're finding yourself spending a lot of time with customer conversations and selling and everything you need to do to drive income into your business, what you need to do is scale that and you scale that by creating a podcast, which allows for more people to listen to you, which allows more people to make a decision on you, makes a small percentage of those people want to connect with you and BOOM.

You have restricted all those discovery calls and all that social media stuff to allow yourself to have so much free time and make a lot of money too.

I have trained quite a few people that were saying they were a seven day a week business and just through the process of podcasting, they have reduced it down to three days, leaving themselves four days for their family because people are now connecting with them the easy way.

They're not having to sell. ***The sales are coming to them.***

Jon: David, what's the second palpable reward that people are going to get out of this?

Profile Explosion

David: Without a doubt, profile explosion.

Now, you might be wondering what that actually means but I'm somebody now with a huge network that I would never have had without podcasting.

I'm somebody that can, by six degrees of separation connect with literally anyone on earth that I want to speak to.

What you find with podcasting is you build that network doubly quick. People listen to you and they want to connect with you. I get so much traffic through Linkedin because of that. They will actually advise me of people that they think will be good on the show, so that boosts that as well.

Your network becomes your net worth as they say.

Now with that, people listen to you and they see you as an expert. I will give you an example of that.

I recorded Join Up Dots episode one and after that first episode, a lady connected with me from Arkansas and said, "David, I love your podcast. I would really like you to coach me in business."

At that time, I knew nothing about business. I was a complete newbie and all I did was record a podcast episode, but they saw me as an expert. Now I've spoken to the Jack Canfields and the huge business people out there. People then connect me with those and they see you on the same level.

Now, you may be, you may not be but it doesn't matter. It's how people see you, so your profile just goes up in record time.

There's about 10 amazing benefits away from the financial element of a podcast, that a podcast brings to your business and you can't get away from the fact that the profile explosion occurs in record time.

I probably have shaved off maybe 15 to 20 years due to what I have done in podcasting, instead of blogging for example, due to the fact that these people are waiting to talk to me.

Also, the other one I suppose is the free coaching.

You talk to these people that would charge thousands and thousands for an hour of their time and they do it for free.

I now say that I've had 1000 business coaches that have taught me.

Through every conversation I have with them, I think to myself, that was a good idea. I hadn't thought of that, or yes, I'm doing that. It really fast tracks your business.

You are surrounding yourself with success. ***Profile explosion is huge.***

Speaking Opportunities

Jon: Of course, David, speaking
        opportunities in business, is
        obviously something we should all
        want, yes?

David: Dependent on your thing to be
        honest. I know some people that
        the thought of actually standing up
        and speaking on anything is a
        complete nightmare. I know some
        podcasters that don't do that at all.
        But it is a great way of bringing
        income in and the bigger audience,
        the more money you get and the
        more exposure, which then means
        your podcast will grow. It's a great
        win/win.

        The beauty of it is, after a while,
        you will have your subject. You
        will know your subject inside out.

If somebody asks me to stand up and talk about podcasting, then limit me for three hours because I'm going to go on forever.

People will want your knowledge base. They will want your information. They will want your profile.

I've done some public speaking. I used to do it all the time and when I started Join Up Dots, I ran away from it because I thought I used to do that all the time. I don't want to do this anymore.

Through the show though, I've done bits and bobs. I've even skyped into the Northern Californian Speakers' Association, so they beamed me in from Skype to actually speak to the audience at that time.

Opportunity is everywhere but you're not going to get those opportunities unless the profile explosion occurs first. You're not going to get that profile explosion unless you start podcasting, so it all works hand in hand.

Jon: Would you say that besides speaking opportunities, it brings a lot more opportunities for different flows of income?

David: Yeah, absolutely. I never dreamt that I was going to do a book and here I am doing book!

I have had joint ventures come through to me. It just happens all the time.

What you've got to be selective on is the joint ventures. I turn down a lot of stuff because I realise people are using my profile more than I want their profile, so I'm very selective on what I get involved with.

With this, I could just see that Jonathan was a class act, that the book was going to be good. I could see the need for it, so it was an opportunity that came to me and I grabbed it with both hands.

You've got to be selective. Once your profile explodes, people will see you as a golden ticket and that golden ticket might be right for them but it's not necessarily right for you or your listener.

Every time, I always think about my listeners and if it's going to be good for them, I will do it, and if it's not, even if it's millions of pounds, I turn it away.

Jon: David Ralph, thanks so much for
            that.

David: Lovely. Thanks very much for
            having me on, Jon. It's been an
            absolute delight to be here.

Jon: And I hope I'm not labouring the
            point, even though… I'm
            labouring the point… but our
            readers and audience of
            entrepreneurs and business owners
            and of course anyone else who's
            reading this or listening to it, or
            indeed watching your videos
            online, will no doubt be very
            interested in finding out even
            more, so let's tell people where to
            find you.

            Mostly of course, they can as I do,
            just listen to Join Up Dots podcast,
            where the good podcasts live and
            that's almost daily.

David: Of course. Of course, there's a
           course at:
           Podcastersmastery.com, which is
           my mastery group based on
           Facebook. Tutorials, Videos and
           stuff and people can register to
           find out about that on the website.

           They get a free training master class
           with me there, and also gain access
           to a *fifteen-part free video course*
           showing how to start a podcast.

           Of course, you can go to
           HypnoArts.com/books, so there's
           a load of different ways that they
           can connect.

Jon: Thank you very much, David. I'm
           sure we'll talk some more.

Meet David

David lives in Essex with his family living the life of his dreams podcasting, away from the corporate world where he started working.

He became a Group Training Manager for Hood Group Ltd. presenting soft skills, key skills and compliance training in Banking and Insurance, and before that as a Sales and Service Manager for National Westminster Bank, he won the regional award for increasing the ROI by 256% for three years running. He also became a popular keynote speaker in and around the city of London.

Now, he records podcasts from his studio at the back of his garden and he enjoys pub lunches and watching Netflix in the afternoon.

Postword

Hi there, it's Jonathan Chase.

I'm incredibly lucky because as Director and Interviewer for HypnoArts Partnership Publishing, I'm allowed to be the facilitator to some awesome people's ideas, expertise and treasures being shared with the world.

David Ralph is a brilliant orator. Chatty and genuinely eager to impart his knowledge about the medium that he loves and feels comfortable with, bringing his years of knowledge and passion, to be the inspiration and motivation in people's lives.

Podcasting is without doubt the up-coming source of knowledge and comfort in this increasingly technological age, it's almost like we have come full circle back to a modern day listening society, where we can listen on the move, in the car, in the bath, and even cooking. David in this book has shown us how easy and satisfying it can be to grow an audience that understands where you are coming from so they connect easily and become part of your life. Read and listen to David and let him help you to find your celebrity voice.

Envoi: This is a 'Postword'.

Unlike a foreword I'm not here to tell you to read the book; I'm here to tell you to read it again, and again.

As with all #HypnoArtsBooks you should be able to do that on an average commute into town, definitely while you're waiting for your cancelled flight, or over a couple of lunches.

Our authors don't do fluff or fancy passages full of rhetoric, we don't do the 'bigger the book the better the content' thing.

So, go back and read it again. Make notes in the margins. Fold page corners to mark the best bits. Spill coffee and tea on the cover...

READ the book and allow it to help your life change. Enhance Your Experience and boost your business now.

HypnoArts Publications

Enhancing the Experience of Life

For the most up to date information on;
Books, Audio, Courses and Video Tutorials,
Author information, links to forums
and FaceBook groups
Live Author Appearances and Events
Visit **HypnoArts.com**

We look forward to meeting you.
Jane Bregazzi. CEO HypnoArts

NOTES

www.ingramcontent.com/pod-product-compliance
Lightning Source LLC
Chambersburg PA
CBHW060611200326
41521CB00007B/742